POWER FOR THE PLANET

Anne Flounders

RED
CHAIR
·PRESS·

Please visit our website at **www.redchairpress.com**.
Find a free catalog of all our high-quality products for young readers.

Power for the Planet

Publisher's Cataloging-In-Publication Data
(Prepared by The Donohue Group, Inc.)

Flounders, Anne.

Power for the planet / Anne Flounders.
p. : ill., maps ; cm. -- (Our green Earth)
Summary: Scientists tell us that some of the fuels that keep our homes and businesses running, power our transportation, and keep us safe are hurting the Earth. Learn why energy companies are working to come up with cleaner ways to supply oil and gas, how fuels in the future will be safer for Earth, and what you can do now to use energy wisely. Includes step-by-step ideas for taking action, different points of view, an up-close look at relevant careers, and more.
Includes bibliographical references and index.
ISBN: 978-1-939656-45-2 (lib. binding/hardcover)
ISBN: 978-1-939656-33-9 (pbk.)
ISBN: 978-1-939656-52-0 (eBook)
1. Fossil fuels--Environmental aspects--Juvenile literature. 2. Energy development--Environmental aspects--Juvenile literature. 3. Energy conservation--Juvenile literature. 4. Fossil fuels--Environmental aspects. 5. Energy development--Environmental aspects. 6. Energy conservation. I. Title.
TD195.E49 F56 2014

333.79/16   2013937164

Illustration credits: p. 6, 12: Joe LeMonnier

Photo credits: Cover, title page, TOC, p. 4, 5, 7, 8, 10, 11, 13, 14, 15, 17, 18, 19, 20, 21, 22, 24, 25, 27, 28, 31, back cover: Shutterstock; p. 16: Michael Starner; p. 17: Michael Fredericks; p. 23: Catherine Divis/OSU-Oklahoma City; p. 25: Richard Hutchings; p. 26: © Dazzo, Alamy; p. 28: Lisa Daniels; p. 32: © Hildi Todrin, Crane Song Photography

This series first published by:
Red Chair Press LLC   PO Box 333   South Egremont, MA 01258-0333

Printed in the United States of America

1 2 3 4 5 18 17 16 15 14

MIX
Paper from
responsible sources
FSC
www.fsc.org   FSC® C002589

Table of Contents

CHAPTER ONE

All About Energy

What do all people use every moment of every day? Energy! Energy makes everything happen. We use our own energy to move, talk, and think. When we need more energy, we fuel our bodies with food and sleep. And it is energy that gives us the food we eat and the beds we sleep in. The sun's energy helps grow plants and trees for food and materials.

Energy is all around us.

People use energy in lots of different ways. Energy powers homes and cars. Energy is used to make anything from paper clips to rocket ships. Energy helps people, animals, and plants stay warm or cool, both indoors and out.

Energy cannot be created or destroyed. It just gets reused. In fact, there is so much energy all around that there is no way to capture and use it all. In a single minute, the sun gives off enough energy to power the whole world for an entire year![1]

There are two kinds of energy. Potential energy is stored until it is ready to be used. Fuel is potential energy. It is energy stored in things like gasoline, coal, and wood. When burned, fuel becomes kinetic energy. Kinetic energy is energy in action, such as electricity, light, and movement.

[1] Source: American Solar Energy Institute

At rest, the bike has potential, or stored, energy. As the bike rolls down the hill, the action becomes kinetic energy.

Potential Energy

Kinetic Energy

Super-heated water erupts from Strokkur Geyser, Iceland.

Where do we get the energy that we use? Energy can be captured from many different sources. The sun provides solar energy. We capture the energy of blowing wind and flowing water. Heat deep inside Earth is a source of **geothermal** energy. The energy from an atom is called nuclear energy.

All of these are renewable forms of energy. They will always be available to use. Other sources of energy are not renewable. These are called **fossil fuels**.

DID YOU KNOW?
Almost all energy we use originated in the sun. We use energy directly from the sun when we capture solar and wind power.

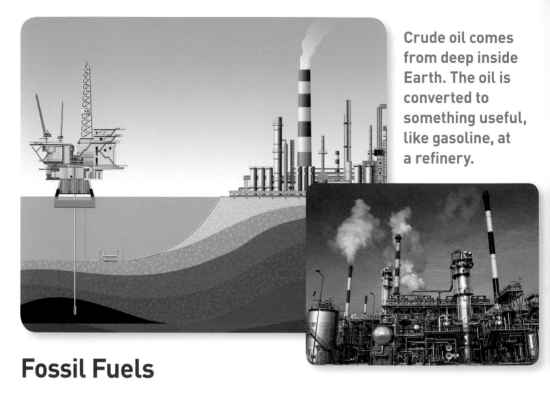

Crude oil comes from deep inside Earth. The oil is converted to something useful, like gasoline, at a refinery.

Fossil Fuels

Most people rely on fossil fuels to power their lives. What are fossil fuels? They are fuels that come from deep inside the Earth. Coal, oil, and natural gas are fossil fuels. We can burn these fuels to release their energy. Fossil fuels were formed from the decaying matter of animals and plants that lived millions of years ago.

Fossil fuels have been a useful source of power for more than 200 years. But fossil fuels will run out one day. In the one hundred years between 1870 and 1970, the world's people used about ten percent of the **crude oil** available in the Earth's crust. Since 1970, people have used that same amount of oil every ten years.[2]

[2] Source: UNESCO

coal

Most households, businesses, and vehicles in the United States are powered by fossil fuels. How do we get them? Where do they come from?

Sound waves are used to locate oil and natural gas deep within Earth. Drills are sent down deep inside the Earth to extract the fuels. Sometimes a solid layer of rock comes between a drill and fossil fuels. In that case, a process called **fracturing** may used to break through rock to get to oil and gas. Coal is mined from the ground using large machines. Coal can be mined on the surface of the ground or deep underground.

Most of the oil we use in the U.S. comes from other nations. We supply most of our own coal and natural gas. A great deal of land is needed to extract these fuels.

Energy We Use

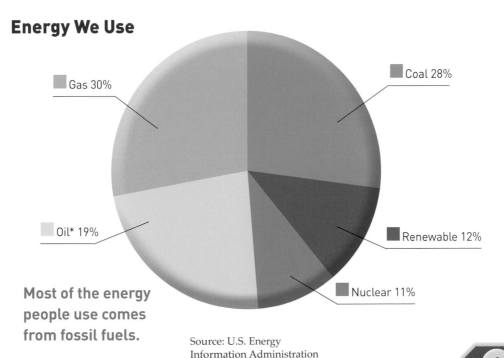

Gas 30%

Coal 28%

Oil* 19%

Renewable 12%

Nuclear 11%

Most of the energy people use comes from fossil fuels.

Source: U.S. Energy Information Administration

Scientists now tell us that the way people get and use fossil fuels has been harmful to our planet. Taking fossil fuels out of the Earth can lead to water and land pollution. Once an area is drilled or mined, it often cannot be used for anything else. Burning fossil fuels, such as coal and oil, can add to air pollution.

Coal is mined in over 50 countries.

When fossil fuels burn, they release **carbon dioxide** into the air. Too much carbon dioxide in Earth's atmosphere can lead to big problems. These may include longer droughts, severe storms, and rising ocean levels. But by getting and using power in different ways, people can help solve those problems.

Air pollution can kill young trees and plants.

Finding a Solution

Many people are working to bring more clean energy to America's power grid. Some energy companies are working hard to come up with cleaner ways to supply oil and gas. The government is investing in many clean energy operations. Some operations are large in scale and can provide clean power to thousands of homes. Some projects are small and will power individual schools and businesses.

Many large businesses are also committed to clean, **renewable** energy. It's good for business, as it will save companies money over time. Customers often like to buy from companies that are green – or good for Earth. Big companies are also very visible to others. If they make big changes in the way they capture and use energy, other businesses may follow their example.

Scientists are looking for ways to make energy safer for Earth. Until they do, people can take simple steps to **conserve** energy. Some ways of using energy are green. And more of the energy we use in the future may come from renewable sources like the sun or wind. That means the energy will always be there and never run out. Now that's green!

experimental solar car

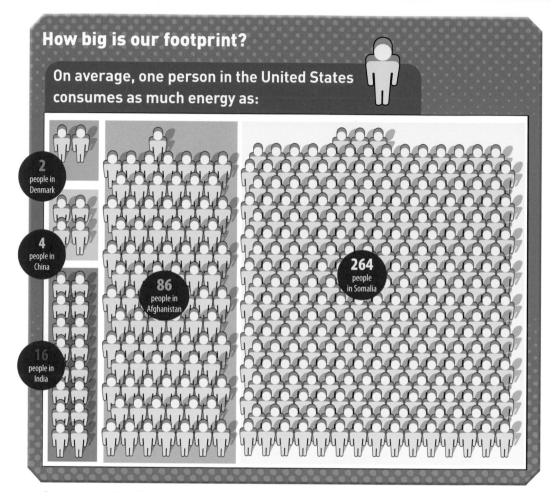

How big is our footprint?

On average, one person in the United States consumes as much energy as:

2 people in Denmark

4 people in China

16 people in India

86 people in Afghanistan

264 people in Somalia

Source: International Energy Annual, 2009 data, U.S. Department of Energy

People can also help by watching their carbon footprints. That is the amount of carbon dioxide emitted by all that you do. Riding in a car, using a computer, and eating a hamburger contribute to your carbon footprint. It takes energy to do all these things. Watching TV for two hours or riding in a car for a mile adds one pound of carbon dioxide to your footprint. If you lower your carbon footprint, you do less harm to Earth.

FACE OFF: Natural Gas

It's a fact: The United States has natural gas deep below its land.

"Natural gas is right here, under our feet! And it's cleaner than coal or oil. We have enough natural gas in the U.S. for all our needs right now. We need to find new ways to use more natural gas for cars, homes, and schools."

Many people like the idea of using more natural gas. There is enough to provide all the energy the United States needs for the present time. That means the U.S. would not depend on bringing fuel in from other countries. Natural gas could provide heat and electricity for millions of homes and businesses and could fuel transportation. Its carbon dioxide emissions are lower than that of oil or coal. That means it could contribute less to climate change. Many see it as a "bridge" between today's use of fossil fuel and a future powered by renewable energy.

"The future of the planet is at stake! I think we should concentrate on increasing our use of clean energy, rather than continuing to drill for gas."

On the other hand, natural gas is still a limited resource. Once it runs out, it's gone. To reach more natural gas, energy companies need to drill along the coasts, in wildlife reserves, and in populated areas. Many people feel the risks of polluting farmland, drinking water, and scenic coasts and land is too high. It can be very expensive to increase production of natural gas. Some people think the money would be better spent to develop renewable energy even if it takes many more years.

What do you think?

CHAPTER TWO

Using Energy Wisely

In our world today, people cannot entirely avoid using fossil fuels. For example, almost all cars use fossil fuels, and people need cars to get to work and other places they need to go. But thirty kids riding one school bus is a greener, more efficient choice than having thirty cars drive kids to school. People agree it is a good idea to be careful about how fossil fuel is used.

CARPOOL

2 OR MORE PERSONS

Transportation is the biggest source of Earth's air pollution.

Great Green Ideas

People work hard to find new ways to use energy wisely. That is, they want to get a job done, such as heating a room, using the least amount of energy possible to get the job done well.

Many schools are using energy in smart ways. For example, some school districts have passed a rule about school buses and their engines. School buses in those districts are not allowed to sit outside schools with their engines running, which is called idling. Idling causes air pollution. If drivers turn off their buses when they arrive at school, they will help keep the air around the school clean. That keeps everyone healthier. Idling is also a waste of fuel. Turning off the bus is an easy way to conserve fuel.

COOL SCHOOL

Schools across America are using sky-high spaces to help them go green! On the "green roof" of Hillside Elementary School in Pennsylvania, flowering plants grow in garden plots. Green roofs act as a natural temperature controller for the school. Rooms under the roof are cooler in warm weather and warmer in cool weather. The green roof reduces the need for energy to heat and cool the school. Students at the school use the green roof as a living science classroom, too!

Architects designed this house to capture rainwater for plants.

Architects and builders have great green ideas, too. They are designing and constructing new houses and buildings that use less energy. Green buildings help their occupants keep lower carbon footprints.

For example, a home may be built to use natural light for heating and cooling. It may have better insulation than a standard house. Insulation keeps the indoor temperature comfortable. That home might use up to 40 to 90 percent less energy for heating and cooling than a standard house. Natural lighting from the sun also reduces the need for electric lighting. The sun's energy is used for hot water and electricity. Green buildings also use energy-saving appliances. And they are built using sustainable or recycled materials.

This Passive House in New York's Hudson Valley uses 90% less energy than a traditional house.

Energy at Home

In the winter, people turn on the heat to stay warm and cozy. In the heat of summer, some people use air conditioning to cool off. Heating and cooling a home are important. Most of the energy people use at home is used for heating and cooling.

Home heat often comes from burning fuel such as oil or natural gas. Home heating systems also heat water for bathing and for washing dishes and clothes. Cooling systems usually run on electricity. Electricity comes from burning coal or other fossil fuels at power stations. The energy is stored until it is delivered in lines to houses and buildings.

It's hard to avoid using home heat and air conditioning. But people can conserve energy by heating and cooling homes only when it is truly needed.

ONE POWERFUL LIST

✔ Turn off lights and appliances when you are not using them.

✔ Unplug less frequently used appliances when they are not in use.

✔ When you aren't using your computer for 20 minutes or more, put it in "sleep" mode. If you aren't going to use your computer for two hours or more, just shut it down.

DO IT!

Smart Energy Use at Home

Kids have the power to conserve energy, too! The whole family can get in on the act of making a home into a clean, green machine. Every act of energy conservation adds up to a big difference for the planet. Three important things to remember are the three Rs.

Reduce the amount of stuff used. Energy is used make things and to dispose of them. Using only what is really needed can help save energy.

Reuse old things so they don't have to be thrown away. Give unwanted clothes and other goods to people who need them.

Recycle paper, cardboard, plastic, and metal. These can be made into other things.

✔ Plug computers and electronic devices into a power strip. When devices are not in use, turn the power strip off.

✔ Turn off the water while you brush your teeth.

✔ Wash clothes in cold water. Clothes get as clean, and the water doesn't need to heat up.

✔ On sunny days, hang laundry outside to dry instead of using the dryer.

CHAPTER THREE

The Sun and the Wind

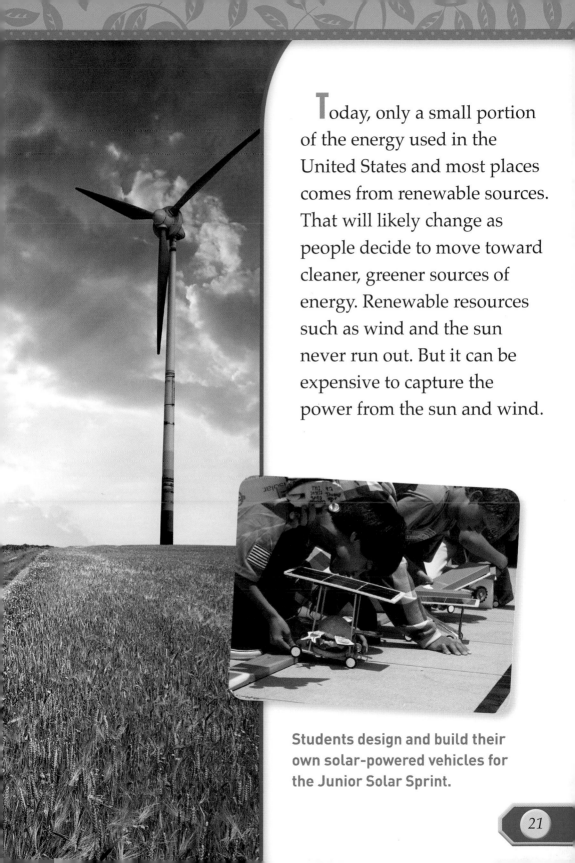

Today, only a small portion of the energy used in the United States and most places comes from renewable sources. That will likely change as people decide to move toward cleaner, greener sources of energy. Renewable resources such as wind and the sun never run out. But it can be expensive to capture the power from the sun and wind.

Students design and build their own solar-powered vehicles for the Junior Solar Sprint.

Solar Power

Using solar energy is a really bright idea! Our sun constantly beams out enormous amounts of energy. In just one second, the sun gives more energy than anyone has ever used in the history of time![3]

Energy from the sun is called **solar power**. The sun's rays can be captured and turned into electricity or heat. Solar batteries can store the sun's energy. These batteries can power anything from a watch to a water heater.

The sun's energy is powerful, plentiful, and free to use. Capturing and using solar energy does not cause pollution. It is a truly clean form of power.

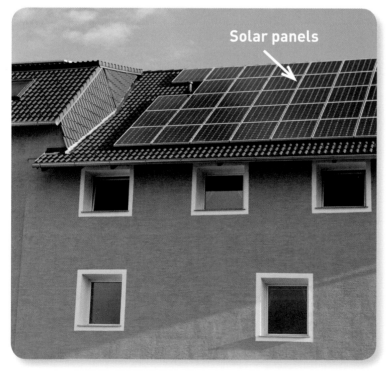

Solar panels

The roof on this house has panels that capture sunlight. The sun's energy is used to make electricity.

[3] Source: Solar Energy International

Do you think you might be interested in a career in sustainable energy or environmental design?

Here are just a few of the jobs you could do.

Construction Manager   *Energy Engineer*
Environmental Scientist *Software Designer*
Solar Project Manager

As a renewable and sustainable energy major, Caleb Manning helped build an energy-efficient parking garage at Oklahoma State University – Oklahoma City. Caleb's advice for students: "Go to class and ask questions. And focus on math skills. Try to get experiences outside of class, too. Working in green construction as a student will give my career a great start!"

CALEB MANNING

Solar energy is becoming more popular in the United States. Many new buildings use solar power. But using solar power is not a new idea. Thousands of years ago, people captured the sun's energy using magnifying glass. That is how they lit fires. Many early cultures also built their homes to capture the natural light and heat of the sun. In 1954, a laboratory in the United States started building solar cells. On April 26, 1954, a front-page article in *The New York Times* declared the solar cell "the beginning of a new era, ...the harnessing of the almost limitless energy of the sun."

If solar energy is so great, why isn't it used more widely? One reason is cost. Even though the sun's rays are free, solar energy systems can be costly to set up. Solar panels and solar collectors grab the sun's energy and convert it into electricity and heat. Another issue is that the sun's rays radiate far and wide. Huge surface areas are needed to capture a useful amount of energy. People are working on ways to make solar power more practical, affordable, and widely available.

Large solar farms or solar energy plants make power for many people. The mirrors move to follow the sun all day.

S'MORE SOLAR

You can make your own solar oven! Just follow these steps. But be careful. Even this simple oven can heat up to 250 degrees F (121 degrees C).

Step 1: Start with a clean pizza box. Cut three sides of a square out of the top of the box. Fold back the flap and cover it in aluminum foil.

Step 2: Cover the inside bottom of the box with black construction paper.

Step 3: Roll up four pieces of newspaper and place them around the inside of the box (one roll along each side). The newspaper helps keep the food warm while it cooks.

Step 4: Place a graham cracker topped with a piece of chocolate and some mini-marshmallows on top of the paper. Then, stretch clear plastic wrap across the top of the cooking area. Stretch it tightly! Close the lid of the box, keeping the foil-lined flap open.

Step 5: Place the box in the sun so that the foil flap is facing the sunlight. The foil directs the heat into the box while the black paper captures it. Watch your s'more heat up. Now you're cooking with solar!

Wind Energy

Anyone who has been in a windstorm knows that the wind has a lot of power. Wind is a promising source of clean, renewable energy. There's enough wind whipping across the United States to produce ten times the amount of energy the country needs if we could catch it.[4]

Machines called **wind turbines** take energy from the moving wind and turn it into electricity. A single wind turbine can create enough electricity to power about 1,000 homes. Large groups of wind turbines are called wind farms.

There are few drawbacks to using wind power. It is clean and plentiful. Wind farms can be set up in out-of-the-way, open areas with low population. They can even be placed on the ocean! But setting up wind farms to capture the power of wind can be expensive today. Still, countries around the world are exploring how to use more wind power.

The Alta Wind Energy Center, opened in southern California in 2012, is the largest wind farm in the United States. The clean energy it produces replaces the air pollution caused by burning fossil fuels—as much as if 446,000 cars were taken off the road!

[4] Source: Wind Energy Foundation

Germany is one country that is moving toward using more renewable energy sources such as wind and solar. By 2020, nearly one-third of that country's electricity will be produced by renewable energy.

Windmills have been used to produce energy for hundreds of years. Today, this old windmill stands alongside modern wind turbines in Germany.

A Powerful Future

Imagine a world with cleaner air, healthier people and plants, and greener land. Cars, trucks, buses, and trains will run on electricity that comes from renewable sources. We may live in that world one day.

In the meantime, saving energy is a great way to be kind to our Earth. Every day, we make decisions that seem small, but are very important in the bigger picture. "Should I recycle this paper?" "Could I turn off this light?"

People are learning to make thoughtful decisions to make sure that our planet stays clean and green for years to come.

Name: Lisa Daniels

Job: Founder and Executive Director of Windustry®

Why is wind important?

Lisa Daniels: Wind comes from the Earth heating and cooling at different rates. As long as there's sunshine, there can be wind energy. This is an important concept. We will not always have the oil and gas we're extracting from the Earth right now. There's a limited quantity of that. When we use it, it's gone. That's the opposite of renewable energy. As long as the sun shines, wind and solar energy can be produced.

How did you first become interested in wind as a resource?

LD: I volunteered for a nonprofit organization that worked on renewable energy. I started taking some classes, just out of interest, about wind energy and different renewable energies. I wanted to do what I could to bring attention to wind. It was a type of energy that could be produced from a resource that we were paying almost no attention to at that point.

What led you to start Windustry?

LD: When wind energy first gets started in an area, someone will knock on farmer's door and say, 'I would like to lease your land and put a wind turbine on it.' Farmers had a lot of questions about what this would mean for their farms. They didn't know if they could still grow traditional crops, how much land it would take, or how much time it would take. I got a job putting together answers for the farmers. The more we worked with farmers, the more interested they became in wind energy. They started asking, if other people can come and put a wind turbine on our land, why can't I put my own wind turbine in? Farmers started asking more questions about the economics and about the wind turbines themselves and about how to put a project together from beginning to end. That's how Windustry got started. We put information together in a meaningful way for the people who were becoming more and more interested in wind energy and how to do wind energy projects.

What is your goal with Windustry?

LD: Windustry has always wanted people to become interested in wind energy. We put together as much information as we can so that people can learn about wind energy and how it makes sense for their community, their farm, or their state, so that rules and policy can be made to support wind energy. Every place in the world where there is wind energy, there is policy to support having that wind energy there.

What do you think is the future of wind energy?

LD: We know it's important to move away from fossil fuels. When we burn fossil fuels it creates emissions and those emissions are changing our climate. We need to work toward getting a clean energy system in place. That system is going to include big wind projects, small wind projects, big solar projects, and small solar projects. We need to put together all kinds of renewal energy projects so that it all contributes to a clean energy system. Right now it is still too hard to build a wind project in the U.S. It needs to get easier. It's not the technology. The technology is here and the technology is always improving. It's the will that is missing. I'm doing what I'm doing because I know renewable energy is part of the solution. And I want to be part of the solution as well.

Check it out: windustry.org

GLOSSARY

carbon dioxide CO_2 , heavy gas formed by the burning of organic matter

conserve to use carefully to avoid waste

crude oil oil in its natural state

fossil fuel fuels made from decayed plant and animal matter; these fuels can be liquid (oil), solid (coal), or gas (natural gas) and are burned to produce energy

fracturing a method of breaking rock deep inside Earth to reach oil or natural gas

geothermal energy produced by the internal heat of the Earth

renewable capable of being replaced by the Earth's natural cycles

solar power energy captured from the sun

wind turbine a machine that captures wind and turns it into electricity

FOR MORE INFORMATION

Books

Drummond, Allan. *Energy Island: How One Community Harnessed the Wind and Changed their World.* Farrar, Straus and Giroux, 2011.

Kamkwamba, William and Bryan Mealer. *The Boy Who Harnessed the Wind: Young Readers Edition.* Dial, 2012.

Leedy, Loreen. *The Shocking Truth About Energy.* Holiday House, 2011.

Storad, Conrad J. *Fossil Fuels.* Lerner, 2008.

Web Sites

Energy Kids: *Homework help, information and activities about energy*
www.eia.gov/kids

Energy Star Kids:
Energy facts, challenges, and tips
www.energystar.gov/kids

All web addresses (URLs) have been reviewed carefully by our editors. Web sites change, however, and we cannot guarantee that a site's future contents will continue to meet our high standards of quality and educational value.

INDEX

About the Author

Anne Flounders has lots of on-the-job experience writing for kids and teens. She has written and edited magazines, nonfiction books, teachers' guides, reader's theater plays, and web content. She has also recorded narration for audio- and ebooks. Anne protects our green Earth with her husband and son in Connecticut.